Christmas Poetry & Art

Written and Created by Sheri Barrante

Christmas Poetry and Art
Copyright © 2020 by Sheri Barrante
ALL RIGHTS RESERVED.

Cover art *Candy Cane* (2020), by Sheri Barrante, 8" x 10" Mixed Media

Book design by Hitchcock Creative

Published by:

Bayou Publishing
18896 Greenwell Springs Road
Greenwell Springs, LA 70739

www.thepublishedword.com

ISBN 978-1-950398-31-7

Printed on demand in the U.S., the U.K., and Australia
For worldwide distribution

Dedication Page

The love for Christmas has always been a common
sentiment for most that I have met. It has been a
special time, and some of the best memories have
stayed from Christmas with friends and family.

I could not imagine life without Christmas and
want to dedicate this book to all the young children,
old children at heart, and animals and pets too that
absolutely love Christmas around the globe.

- Sheri -

Contents

Part
ONE

Christmas Ribbon with Christmas Tree (2020)
by Sheri Barrante
8" x 10", Mixed Media

God's Glory at Christmas

Christmas is more than another day on the calendar. It is so much more with family and friends that otherwise keep so busy and often have long stays away from each other.

It is a gathering worth coming together for, yet is it because of the hope? Is it because of the joy? Is it because of the receiving another gift? Perhaps one could resolve yes, it is because of all of that wrapped up in one that we call the Messiah, Jesus, A king, a Ruler, yet a humble servant, who loves with love that gifts bigger than Kings, and wiser than the wisest, and yet more humble than the humblest, and more noble than rumors have ever tried to destroy-- it brings love past borders races and nations diseases and illnesses sorrows and losses triumphs and victories sounds and frequencies.

This is the Glory of all Christmas, the Messiah, an everlasting flood of goodness and deliverance. It is most of all that with promises of eternal love and life for you; for all of you that were ever formed, ever created, ever would be, and will forever be under the mist of the glory and the love – at Christmas.

Starry Sky Christmas

There was a twinkle in His eyes, Under a Starry sky

His guests, however, were not the usual kind

Kings had come in from the far East

They were led by a guide a Big Star in the Sky

They had their maps, but the one from above made sure they would

Know the best cartographer

Ever of all, whose GPS was a bright Brilliant Star Guiding from East to West from glories into present day and all our best, timeless and yet current, seamless, genius, and yet worshiped and adored.

It was a party, indeed, the Birth of one from Above, to be celebrated for generations to come

A savior, a friend Who would bear all our sins

Jesus the Christ was His Name

It was His birth we would celebrate and in no less than we call our Christmas Days.

Christmas Winds

Christmas Winds and whirls rushing in for the season

Attentive to details that come along when we approach that date

Even closer towards the end of the year.

It doesn't have to be the North Pole to have some

Jolly on the end of one's nose.

As Christmas winds rushing in to

bring us a nice peaceful wintry snow.

Christmas Eyes

Reflect the Lights

Greens, Reds, Yellows, Whites and Blues

Around Tinsel that cats come and warm up to

Under the greenery with the tree skirt too

A little purring and a little music playing inside
as the snow briskly

Flows down from wintry skies.

These Christmas eyes

w/so much surprise looking just as they do.

Part
TWO

Christmas Angels (2020)
by Sheri Barrante
8" x 10", Mixed Media

Angels Visiting by Christmas Eve

Angels visiting and gliding in for Christmas

For in Worship they are surely in the midst

So many and no shortage of them

Plenty for every nation, people and tribe

Perhaps angels of singing, angels of joy,
angels of history, angels of glory

All Rushing In

For the level of worship and adoration increases

Around this Christmas thus bringing angel guests

Even before the Eve of Christmas.

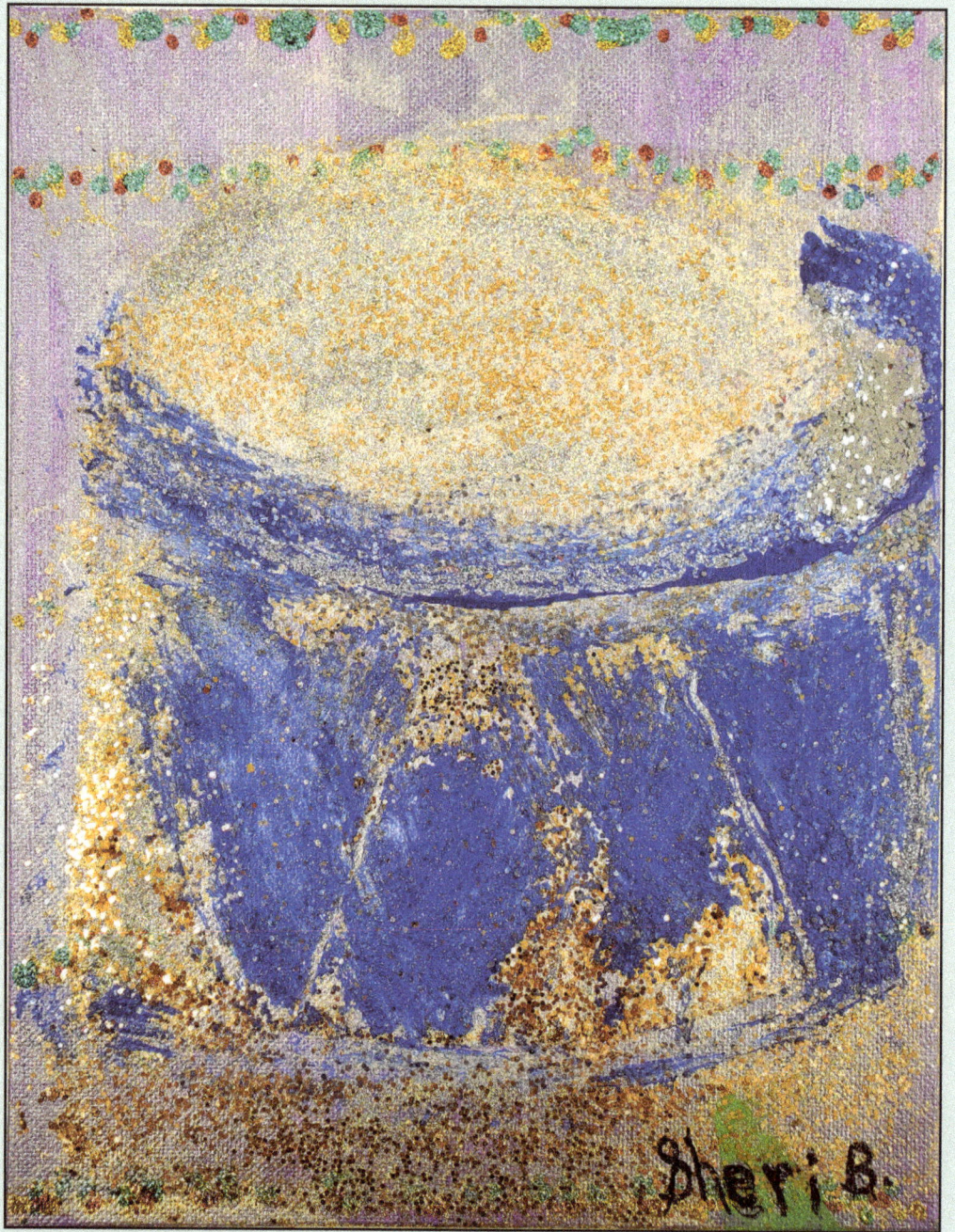

Drummer Boy (2020)
by Sheri Barrante
8" x 10", Mixed Media

Drums, Sheep and Hay

There was a presence in the atmosphere a glory

That calmed the soul and caused every creature to just know

Resting on the very nature of man, that would transform the world in an eternal pivot

With sounds and sights that would never leave history's nights even into this hour and day

The drummer boy would play his song, the animals would keep it to soft lulls, as if all stood still, that even more the world would know that a King had the center of this show, and amongst drums sheep and hay,

The common was undone with the spectacular through the simplest and humblest acts of love this world has ever been shown.

Ice Snow (2020)
by Sheri Barrante
8" x 10", Mixed Media

The Bells of Christmas

Christmas bells ringing in that old antique town

Children running, and where the old sleighs ran through

Powdered snow, and fireplaces that kept people warm

Churches with incense burning where tradition reigned down cloudy smoke from frankincense and myrrh

As the hallelujahs sound and the snow whirls outside around the door frames

The windows are glazed with icy patterns and it is all okay

As the service carries on amongst sounds of the oldest of hymns being hummed telling of a saviors birth along with Christmas bells that were rung.

Part THREE

Snow Skiers (2020)
by Sheri Barrante
8" x 8", Mixed Media

Snow Shoes and Snowy Skies

Snow Shoes and Snowy Skies

On a Cheery Day

With Travel and play

A cottage on a Hill and a Chalet

In there Hot Cocoa is certainly on the way

Marshmallow Whip

Sports Jackets and Sporty Fur Hats

Mittens and Stows

Where Happy Clatter Surrounds wooden stoves

And the Warmth of Fireplaces Amongst Cheery Relatives Overlooking

All the Grandeur.

Candy Canes (2020)
by Sheri Barrante
8" x 10", Mixed Media

Candy Canes

Candy canes and Christmas treasures

in Cedar boxes with red and green ribbon arrived

Smiles quickly traveled as grandma gave a big grin.

The family in Route including Aunts, Uncles, and cousins to visit

Showers of hugs, before major Christmas traditions would begin.

Christmas cheer was found even amongst puppies,

Guys and gals walking by Candlelight services

As Christmas was more and more through the aromatic smells of evergreens and the fresh evening air.

Christmas Camels (2020)
by Sheri Barrante
8" x 10", Mixed Media

Christmas Camels

Adorned and heavily weighed

With Those long lashed eyes would be walking under brilliant night skies

The sands would be cooler yet these Camels would be arrayed with finest of purple, silk and cloths with intense focus on the following of a star, with their precious boxes of gold, silver, frankincense and myrrh, They were quite brilliant

Shining under the light from the Eastern star. Other creatures were also out and about, yet, none were arrayed quite as marvelously as these and ridden by wise men some considered to be kings.

Christmas Sailboats (2020)
by Sheri Barrante
8" x 10", Mixed Media

Christmas Journey

A Christmas journey where the family set sail for a sunny island

way past the noise and pollution.

Sailing in the deep seas, we left from a port and from a sandy beach for our wintry vacation

Setting for nautical miles where the sun and warmth

would bring us to sandy whites and memories of what it must have been like when

three wise men set out also across sand, loaded down with anticipation

we for our long awaited vacation, and the wise men of the event for meeting

Jesus the King.

Soon the city was far behind us on the vessel, there was plenty to set our eyes on –

could see miles and miles amongst low lying waves and occasionally a fish jumping

through the ocean waves. The sea gulls were singing their own songs

As we contemplated Christmas amongst the ocean gales and fervent sea sounds as we set sail for the port w/Christmas lights and wintry Christmas sights.

Christmas Birds (2020)
by Sheri Barrante
8" x 10", Mixed Media

Colors, Wingspreads
Before Holiday Cheer

Birds with red, blues, and sunshine yellows, flew in

    With Beautiful Wingspreads, a forest chatter of song

A focus view of a partial globe shadowed by slight sparkling white mist coming down,

A cardinal on the short branch of that tall tree overseeing everything.

    There must be bedtime stories amongst even God's creatures.

It is as if the creatures of flight knew the Holidays, Thanksgiving and Christmas

    Were being brought on the winds of cooler breezes.

Now it was time for three strong men and a half-ton truck

    and a healthy stack of wood for the fire place.

Joyful songs and colors arrayed in the late wintry air.

    Bird seed arriving, stacks of firewood, cooler days only an anticipation

before holiday cheer

Part
FOUR

Cross (2020)
by Sheri Barrante
8" x 10", Mixed Media

Christmas Boldness

Come Oh My Soul, Rise up and tell of all

Dance Sing, Cry and Twirl

Come oh with Streaks of Joy

Erasing the skating edges of the old

The Story of Jesus Blazes on

The Love of the Father, Son, Holy Spirit in One

Oh, Let the Eternal King Victoriously Proclaim

Through a Child's Laughter, a Pluck of a String, a Note sent through

Waves in the Air, a Dance, a Leap, a Twirl, a Smile, a Kind Word,

An Everlasting Hug, on a Lonesome Day

Oh, My Savior who Reigns

With Christmas Boldness, Come, Oh My Soul, and Tell All of a King Who Lives On!

Kingly Rights

To spread Christmas around the world

Through a majestic baby 1st hidden in a momma's womb.

Then tucked in a manger oh King Herod, it would be too late when he would know

There were other kings that would make this event full

A poured out sacrifice into a sleepy world

As worship would spread around the globe as He the King of Kings

poured out like pressed oil and worship would arise

As an incense the very likeness of the Father, the very sovereign Lord, more than an image God on earth in the form of a man, yet with power to heal, and reveal, that He was a heavenly King.

He Himself, on Earth to bring Kingly Rule from a Kingdom not of this world

Jesus the Messiah would soon be more than a household name, He Himself would be shared through Christmas songs and for the eternal life He alone brings.

A tear of Joy
in the Drop of the World

Laughter to solace the poor wonderer and warmth for the coldest of souls

In palaces and in the poorest of spaces, the invitation Remains

A Savior came, all are welcome in

From this country to that all are invited to know

Jesus came to save us from sins

We just have to invite Him In,

One day the trumpets will sound and the skies will open

He will remember

On that day His grace will remain

A celebration, He in His Royal Robe

Christmas is merely a Preview

For the Greater we are about to Know.

Conclusion

Christmas is a festive and fun time of the year. And yet also there is an underlying hint for the one curious that would say Who is this Jesus? And Do you know Him? Because you can know Him. You can ask Him to come into your heart. You can ask Jesus Christ to come into your life and forgive all your sins to wash your soul clean and bring you into salvation. You can be confident of this that He is faithful, that He will forgive your sins if you ask Him and that He loves you and wants you to know Him. Today is the day, if you have said yes, and invited Him in your heart, find a special place and write down this special date. In addition, find a minister, pastor or priest in a church to help you to know what to do next. And a great big Congratulations and welcome to the Family of God.

Todays Date: _____

www.ingramcontent.com/pod-product-compliance
Lightning Source LLC
Chambersburg PA
CBHW040856100426
42813CB00015B/2818